JACKIE ROBINSON

Strong
Inside and Out

By the Editors of TIME FOR KIDS
WITH DENISE LEWIS PATRICK

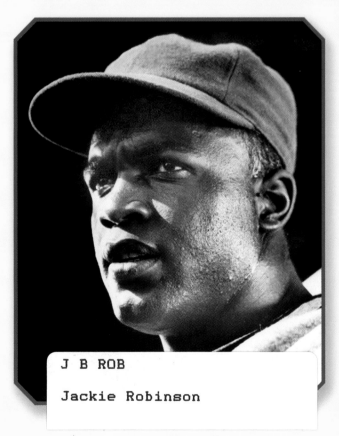

J B ROB

Jackie Robinson

HarperCollinsPublishers

About the Author: "Reading has always been as great a passion for me as writing is," says Denise Lewis Patrick, a native of Natchitoches, Louisiana. Author of more than twenty-five books for young people, she lives in New Jersey with her husband and their four sons.

LIBRARY OF CONGRESS CATALOGING-IN-PUBLICATION DATA
Jackie Robinson : strong inside and out / by the editors of Time for Kids with Denise Lewis Patrick.— 1st ed.
p. cm.
ISBN 0-06-057600-6 (pbk.) — ISBN 0-06-057601-4 (trade)
1. Robinson, Jackie, 1919–1972—Juvenile literature. 2. Baseball players—United States—Biography—Juvenile literature. 3. African American baseball players—Biography—Juvenile literature. [1. Robinson, Jackie, 1919–1972. 2. Baseball players. 3. African Americans—Biography.] I. Patrick, Denise Lewis. II. Time for kids online.
GV865.R6J35 2005   2003026427
796.357'092—dc22

1 2 3 4 5 6 7 8 9 10
First Edition

Photography and Illustration Credits:
Cover: Hulton Archive—Getty Images; inset: Sporting News; Time Life Pictures—Getty Images; front flap: Library of Congress; contents page: Time Life Pictures—Getty Images; p. iv: National Baseball Hall of Fame; p. 1: public domain; pp. 2–3: Library of Congress; p. 2: Library of Congress; p. 3 (bottom): Sporting News; p. 4: Jackie Robinson Foundation; p. 5 (bottom left): Photodisc; p.5 (bottom right): Time Life Pictures—Getty Images; Photodisc; p.6: Bettmann-Corbis; pp. 6–7 (top): Photodisc; p. 7 (top): Photodisc; p. 7 (bottom): Jackie Robinson Foundation; p. 8: National Baseball Hall of Fame; p. 9 (top): Photodisc; p. 9 (center): Time Life Picture Collection; p. 10: Hulton Archive—Getty Images; p. 11: Bettmann-Corbis; p. 12: Sporting News; p. 15: Library of Congress; pp. 16–17: AP Photo—Matty Zimmerman; pp. 18–19: Sporting News; p. 20: AP Photo—John J. Lent; p. 21: Jackie Robinson Foundation; p. 23: Sporting News; p. 24: AP Photo; p. 25: Bettmann-Corbis; pp. 26–27: Bettmann-Corbis; p. 28: National Baseball Hall of Fame; p. 29: Time Life Pictures—Getty Images; p. 30: Bettmann-Corbis; p. 31 (inset): Tony Triolo; p. 32 (inset): Photodisc; p. 32 (bottom): AP Photo—Harry Harris; p. 33 (clockwise from bottom left): Time Life Pictures—Getty Images; National Baseball Hall of Fame; courtesy James Beck; p. 34: Bettmann-Corbis; p. 35: Time Life Pictures—Getty Images; p. 36 (inset): Bettmann-Corbis; p. 36 (bottom): AP Photo—Jacob Harris; p. 37: David and Janice L. Frent Collection—Corbis; p. 38 (top left): Bettmann-Corbis; p. 38 (center right): AP Photo; p. 39: AP Photo; p. 40 (top): Bettmann-Corbis; p. 40 (bottom right): Bettmann-Corbis; p. 41 (top): AP Photo—Ruth Fremson; p. 41 (bottom); AP Photo—USPS; p. 42 (center): courtesy of Sharon Robinson; p. 42 (bottom): Ariel Skelley—Corbis; p. 43: Getty Images; p. 44 (top to bottom): Library of Congress; Corbis; Corbis; Time Life Pictures–Getty Images; back cover: Library of Congress

Acknowledgments:
For TIME FOR KIDS: Editorial Director: Keith Garton; Editor: Jonathan Rosenbloom; Art Director: Rachel Smith; Designer: Esta Shapiro; Photography Editor: Sandy Perez

 Find out more at www.timeforkids.com/bio/robinson

CONTENTS

"There's not an American in this country free until every one of us is free."
—JACKIE ROBINSON

Hero on the Field

Jackie Robinson stepped onto the field in his new Brooklyn Dodgers baseball uniform. He was nervous. The crowd roared. Cameras flashed. Reporters scribbled on their notepads. It was 1947. Jack Roosevelt Robinson was the first African American to play baseball for a modern major-league team.

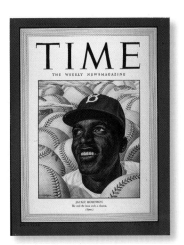

◄ COVER MAN
Robinson was on the cover of the September 22, 1947, issue of TIME magazine. The words under his picture say, "He and his boss took a chance."

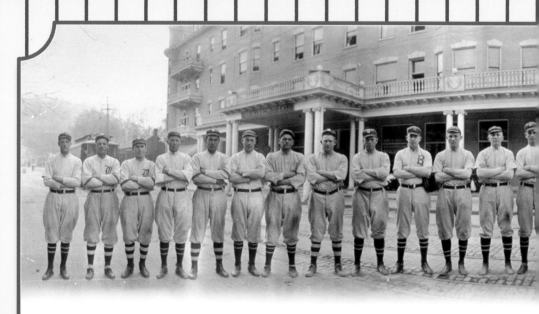

▲ WHITES ONLY
Major-league teams were all white until 1947. This is an early photo of the Dodgers.

He was big news because he was breaking rules. Back in the 1940s, laws in many states told black people where they could live, work, or even eat. The sports world was also segregated. Baseball players who happened to be African American had to play in a league of their own, separate from white players.

Jackie Robinson was about to change all of that.

The Brooklyn Dodgers' owner, Branch Rickey, had warned Jackie of what could happen. Some fans would be angry. Ballplayers might try to hurt him. Some teams

WAITING ROOM
FOR COLORED ONLY
➡
BY ORDER
POLICE DEPT.

◄ SEGREGATION meant keeping blacks and whites apart.

might refuse to compete against a team with a black man. Jackie would have to hold his head up and play the best ball he ever had.

Many people asked that day, "Can he do it? Can he take the hard times and not fight back?"

Jackie Robinson's answer to the world was *yes*! When he walked onto Ebbets Field in Brooklyn, New York, on April 15, 1947, he knew he was ready to handle anything.

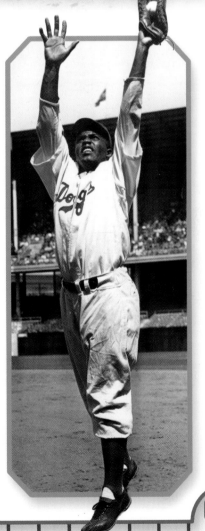

▶ JACKIE makes an out soon after he began playing for the Brooklyn Dodgers.

California
Here I Come

Jackie's mom, Mallie, had taught him to work hard in life and expect good things to happen. That was how Mallie raised all her children. Jackie had three older brothers: Edgar, Frank, and Mack. Willa Mae, his only sister, was two years old when Jackie was born on January 31, 1919. His father, Jerry, left the family soon after. Jackie never saw his dad again.

The family lived on a farm in Cairo, Georgia. Jackie's grandparents, who had been slaves, lived nearby. When Jackie was sixteen months old, Mallie decided to move west. She'd heard there were better jobs for black people in California. So she packed up Jackie, his three brothers, and his sister. A few aunts, uncles, and cousins went, too. The close-knit family took the train from Georgia to Pasadena, California.

The Robinsons were one of the few black families in the city. At first their white neighbors didn't like it when the Robinson kids played outside. Sometimes they called the police, even when the children hadn't done anything wrong! Mallie didn't show any anger. She stayed friendly. Slowly the neighbors got used to one another.

◀ **WE ARE FAMILY**
Jackie is the boy in the hat (second from left). He is shown with his brothers, sister, and his mother, Mallie.

Photographs

▲ **HOME SWEET HOME**
In 1950 Jackie Robinson visited his boyhood home in Pasadena, California. The little boy is Robinson's son Jackie Jr.

Jackie did well in elementary school. He liked to read and spent a lot of time at the library. But as he grew, he liked sports better than anything else. He also began to learn some hard lessons about his hometown. People with dark skin were treated differently from white people.

No Fair!

Hispanics, African Americans, and Asians could use the town's public swimming pool and the local YMCA only one day a week. Jackie and his friends hated such an unfair rule. They decided to fight it the only way they could think of. They sneaked into the reservoir that held the town's water and took a swim. That was against the law, and Jackie and his friends, the Pepper Street Gang, got caught by the town sheriff. He took them to jail. Many folks in Pasadena, including some of the police, thought Jackie might be starting a lifetime of being in trouble.

In high school Jackie tried to be like his brothers. Two of them were natural athletes. His oldest brother, Edgar, was a speed skater. His brother Mack ran track

▲ JUMP UP!
Mack Robinson was a champion broad jumper. This photo was taken in 1937.

at his college, UCLA.

In 1936, when Jackie was still a teenager, Mack made the U.S. Olympic track team. He traveled across the world to Berlin, Germany, for the Olympic Games. Back in California, his family crowded around their radio to follow Mack's races. They cheered as they imagined what the race was like. They knew he had trained hard. His work paid off. He won a silver medal!

Tops in Sports

After that, Jackie began to run track, too. He was excellent at it, just as he was in the other sports he played—basketball, tennis, baseball, and football. But, while Pasadena residents may have cheered for Jackie on his sports teams, the same people didn't allow him to swim in the public pool.

Jackie wanted to go to college, maybe to UCLA. At the same

▲ MAD DASH MACK
Mack Robinson won a silver medal in the 200-meter dash at the 1936 Olympic Games in Germany.

time he thought he should work and help his mother. He decided to start at a small college, Pasadena Junior College. It was closer to home, and it had a sports program. Mack had started there, too.

In 1939, after two years, Jackie moved to UCLA. He became famous on campus, where he ran track and played football, baseball, and basketball. He ran so fast with the football that a newspaper nicknamed him Jack Rabbit Robinson.

It was also at UCLA that he met a girl he liked very much—Rachel Isum, a nursing student. Jackie took classes in French, geometry, and physical education. He began to think about becoming a coach, or maybe even a pro athlete.

Then Jackie's brother Frank died in a motorcycle accident. Frank and Jackie had been very close. Jackie didn't talk much about

▼ RUNS IN THE FAMILY
Jackie, like his brother Mack, was a broad jumper. Here Jackie takes part in a 1939 event at UCLA.

how upset he was. He put his feelings into sports. He played harder than ever.

Jackie Quits

Jackie kept playing football for UCLA, but he lost hope about his future in professional sports. In 1940 there were no black professional football, basketball, or baseball players. Jackie

▲ HELMET ACTION
Jackie (number 28) rushes with the ball. He was the first UCLA athlete to win letters in four sports.

wasn't keeping his grades up. After four years the school rules would not allow him to play sports anymore. He didn't want to stay just to study. He wanted to play sports. His coaches and his girlfriend, Rachel, were against his quitting. They wanted him to work harder on his grades and graduate. But at the end of 1940, Jackie decided to quit college to work full-time.

In 1941 Jackie found a job as a sports director at a youth camp in northern California. He liked working with young people. At the camp he set up games and sports programs. Jackie was starting a new life.

But a whole world away, something else was starting—World War II.

CHAPTER 3

Jackie
Learns to Fight

War changes people's lives everywhere. Jackie's world began to change in big ways. The camp closed and he lost his job. What did he know how to do, other than play football? Jackie heard about a spot on a semi-pro football team called the Honolulu Bears in Hawaii. He went for it and was hired.

When the team's season ended in early December 1941, Jackie sailed back to Los Angeles. His ship left from the port of Pearl Harbor, Hawaii. Two days later Japan bombed the navy base at Pearl Harbor. The United States entered World War II.

Young men were *drafted*, or called to serve in the army. Jackie's job hunt was over—at least for a few years. He became a soldier and went to basic training at Fort Riley, Kansas, in 1942. There he met Joe Louis, the world heavyweight boxing champion. Louis was also doing basic training. Their friendship would last many years.

When basic training was done, Private Robinson was assigned to a unit that cared for horses. He wanted a better job. He thought he could do more.

Black soldiers were allowed to serve only in all-black units. Jackie discovered that white men with the same education could go to officer training school. He could not.

Joe Louis decided to help Jackie. He asked a friend in Washington, D.C., to see what he could do. Pretty soon—maybe because of Joe Louis's buddy, maybe because the army decided to be more fair—Jackie and several other black soldiers were accepted to train to become officers in the army.

▲ FRIENDSHIP
Joe Louis (right) and Jackie Robinson first met in the army. Their friendship lasted for years.

Officer Robinson

Jackie graduated in 1943 with his gold officer's bars. He was now a second lieutenant. He wanted the folks at home to see how well he had done. So he went to Pasadena, wearing his sharp new uniform. Then he visited Rachel in Los Angeles. He asked her to become his wife when he got out of the army. Rachel said yes.

Jackie started his new army job at Fort Hood, Texas. One day he was riding the bus from town back to the base. He took a seat in the middle of the bus. The law in many parts of the country said that African Americans had to sit at the back, or stand up.

Jackie refused to move to the back. The bus driver reported him to the Fort Hood police. He said Jackie had used bad words and started a fight. Jackie was arrested. His case went to an army trial. If he lost, he could be thrown out of the army.

◀ JACKIE JOINS THE FIGHT
Robinson proudly shows off his army uniform.

Luckily some witnesses at the trial told the truth. Yes, he had sat in the middle of the bus, they said. But he had not hit anyone or started trouble. Jackie won his case. But the trial left him unhappy with the army. So he wrote a letter to the Secretary of the Army asking to be let go. He was sent home in 1944.

Once again Jackie went back to sports. Another soldier he'd met played with the Kansas City Monarchs baseball team. The Monarchs were one of the best-known teams in the Negro National League, and they were looking for players. Since Jackie had played baseball in school, he decided to try out for the team.

JACKIE'S WORDS TO LIVE BY

When Jackie became an adult, he thought about how he wanted to live his life. He thought about how he wanted to be treated. And he thought about how he wanted to treat others. He came up with nine values to guide his life. These are his values to live by:

Citizenship: Do good works to help others improve their lives.
Commitment: If you make a promise to do something, be sure to keep your promise.
Courage: Do what you believe is the right thing—no matter how hard it may be.
Determination: Have a goal in mind and stick to it.
Excellence: Do your best at everything you try.
Integrity: Be true to your values and what you believe.
Justice: Be fair to all people.
Persistence: Don't give up on reaching your goals.
Teamwork: Work well with others and cooperate to reach a goal you all share.

CHAPTER 4

Baseball
Makes Jackie a Star

The Negro National League was made up of famous teams such as the Homestead Grays and the Birmingham Black Barons. The Kansas City Monarchs were full of talent. They already had veteran players like pitcher Satchel Paige and outfielder James "Cool Papa" Bell.

A ROYAL PLAYER ▶
In 1945 Robinson played shortstop for the Kansas City Monarchs. The team was part of the Negro League.

Jackie hadn't played serious baseball since his college days. He knew he needed practice. He tried out anyway, hoping to get a spot. The Monarchs decided he was good enough to make the team. Jackie was hired to play shortstop.

The traveling life of the Negro League was hard for Jackie to get used to. Almost every night the team was on the road, playing against a different team in a different town. Some states had laws that kept African Americans and whites apart. This made the team's hard life even harder. The team couldn't enter most restaurants. Sometimes that meant sandwiches and sodas for breakfast. When they did have an extra day or two between games, they had to grab sleep on the bus—unless they

found a hotel or rooming house that would accept African American guests.

Jackie had been with the Monarchs only a short time when some scouts came to watch him play. He and other Negro Leaguers often had been scouted by major-league teams. Nothing had happened. No team seemed ready for—or had players willing to accept— an African American player.

Jackie didn't know it, but a man named Branch Rickey, the Brooklyn Dodgers' owner, had made up his mind to do an experiment.

"IT AIN'T BRAGGING!"

Leroy "Satchel" Paige was never short on words or slow with a baseball. He spent most of his career in the Negro Leagues and was one of the greatest pitchers in history.

Satchel was a country boy from Alabama who became a baseball star with his amazing skills. He loved showing off from the mound. He called his pitches bloopers, loopers, wobblys, and nothin' balls.

Rickey knew that there were fine players in the Negro League who could help the Dodgers win a World Series pennant. He knew it would be difficult. Some other owners might try to stop him. So he pretended he was starting another Negro League— with a team he called the Brown Dodgers. He wanted his plan to remain a secret until he found just the right man.

It was Rickey's scouts who had seen Jackie in 1945. They returned to New York with good reports. Rickey invited Jackie to a meeting.

◄ **KING OF THE MONARCHS**
Paige pitches in a 1942 game against the New York Cuban Stars. Both teams were part of the Negro League.

Crowds packed every stadium where he played. He started with the Chattanooga Lookouts and went to the Kansas City Monarchs in 1939. By then anybody and everybody in baseball had heard of him. He even had pitching contests against white pitchers, like famous Dizzy Dean, who called him "the best pitcher I ever did see."

By the time Jackie Robinson broke the color barrier in the major leagues, Paige was forty-two years old. The Cleveland Indians hired Paige to play in 1948 as the oldest rookie in big-league history. Satchel threw a shutout in a game with the Chicago White Sox and helped the Indians win the American League pennant. Satchel was voted into the Baseball Hall of Fame in 1971. "If you can do it," he said, "it ain't bragging!"

Jackie found out what Branch Rickey was up to when he arrived. Jackie remembered it this way: "When I walked into Mr. Rickey's office, he was puffing on a big cigar. He rose from his leather swivel chair and shook my hand.

"Mr. Rickey got right to the point. 'I think you can

play in the major leagues," he said.

"I was batting over .300, and I had stolen a lot of bases. But there were plenty of older, more established Negro league stars. Why me?

"Mr. Rickey had been looking for a black player who could stand up to taunts from bullies and racists. He thought I was that man.

"Mr. Rickey warned that I would face beanballs (pitches that hit the batter) and fists. He said I would be called dirty names. He told me I'd have to permit all those things to happen and not lose my temper.

"'Mr. Rickey,' I asked, 'are you looking for a Negro who is afraid to fight back?'

"'Robinson,' he rumbled, 'I'm looking for a ballplayer with guts enough *not* to fight back.'"

There were no Brown Dodgers at all, Rickey admitted. Did Jackie want a chance to become a Brooklyn Dodger? Of course! Was he willing to first play for the Montreal Royals, the Dodgers' "farm," or training, team in Canada? Jackie was willing.

Then Rickey went on. What would Jackie do if a white player spat on him? What if white fans booed him or threw things? What if a pitcher tried to hit him with a beanball? All of these things might happen, because many people in 1945 didn't like the idea of whites and blacks playing together on the same team.

▲ ROBINSON in his Montreal Royals uniform gets ready to wow the fans. The Royals were the Dodgers' farm team.

Jackie sat up straighter. Rickey didn't know anything about him. He was strong. He was tough. Jackie Robinson could fight back!

But was he tough enough *not* to fight back? Could Jackie be better than the people who called him names because of his color? Could he ignore people who threw things at him?

Jackie thought about it. He thought of his mother and also his grandmother, who had survived slavery.

They had always reminded him to be proud of being black. They had told him that what mattered most was not what people said about him. What mattered most was trying to be a good person on the inside. Jackie began to understand what was expected of him.

Meeting the Challenge

Jackie knew that if he agreed, he had to show that he was as strong on the inside as he was on the outside. Jackie could prove to the world that the kind of man he was had nothing to do with the color of his skin. He could do two things he had wanted for a long time. He could marry Rachel and play professional ball. Jackie believed he could meet the challenge.

He signed a contract with Rickey to play for the Montreal Royals. If Jackie did well with the Royals, he would move up to the Dodgers—a major-league team in the National League.

◄ WEDDING BELLS
Jackie and Rachel get married. Their good friend Karl Downs performed the ceremony.

Strong
Inside and Out

Traveling in the South on the way to spring training was a challenge for Jackie and Rachel. Because the Robinsons were African American, the airline asked them to give up their seats on one part of their flight to Daytona Beach, Florida. When they finally got on another airplane, the same thing happened again.

Finally an angry Jackie and Rachel took a bus and rode for hours. They sat in the back.

Once they reached Florida, they didn't have a room in the same hotel as the rest of the team. The South's Jim Crow laws forbade black and white people from staying in the same hotels. Already Jackie was being treated differently from the other players.

Jackie couldn't wait to put all this behind him and start training. As weeks

WELCOME HOME! ▶
Jackie is congratulated by a teammate after hitting a home run at his first Montreal game on April 14, 1946.

passed, he sharpened his batting skills and began to fit in with the rest of the team. Rachel came to watch him practice every day. In the Royals' season opener, Jackie hit a home run. His teammates saw that he could help them win. Things were going well.

Wherever the Royals went to play, there was trouble. One team said they would not show up for a game if the Royals brought Jackie. In another town a mob of angry white people came to the field before the game, looking

for Jackie. He and Rachel had to leave town—fast.

At some stadiums angry white fans shouted ugly words and called Jackie awful names. Jackie held his anger inside, but he had trouble sleeping. Sometimes he couldn't eat. When he found out that Rachel was going to have a baby, he also worried about her health.

But somehow, when Jackie played ball, he focused on the game and his playing. He put all other thoughts out of his head.

The Royals had a winning season and headed for the Little World Series against the Louisville Colonels.

DID YOU KNOW?

From the 1880s until the early 1960s, many of the states in the U.S. had laws keeping black and white people separate from one another. The name of the laws came from a white actor who dressed as a black character called Jim Crow. Some called these laws separate but equal. Today we know the laws were separate and unfair. Here are just a few:

▲ UNEQUALS
As recently as the 1960s, blacks and whites had to drink from different water
fountains in many southern states.

Jim Crow Laws

"The state must establish separate waiting rooms at all [train and
bus] stations for the white and colored races...."   North Carolina

"It shall be unlawful to conduct a restaurant at which white and
colored people are served in the same room...."   Alabama

"All circuses and shows shall provide not less than two ticket offices
and two entrances, not less than 25 feet apart...."   Louisiana

"It shall be unlawful for colored people to frequent any park owned by
the city for the use and enjoyment of white people...."   Georgia

"It shall be unlawful for any colored child to attend any white school or
any white child to attend a colored school...."   Missouri

The first games of the series—similar to the major leagues' World Series—were in Kentucky.

It would have been very difficult for Louisville to back out of the series or refuse to play. They agreed to allow Jackie on the field—but they closed part of the black seating section of the stadium so that most black fans couldn't get into the games. An African American player could play—but black fans wouldn't be able to enjoy seeing him. In those days before many people had TVs, this was especially mean.

The Louisville fans were the worst Jackie had ever seen. He went into a batting slump. From time to time during their careers, many players have trouble hitting. For Jackie the timing was horrible. The Royals went back to Montreal, behind, to play the next games.

Cheers for Jackie

It helped that the fans in Montreal loved Jackie. No matter how badly the visiting team or its fans acted toward him, the Royals fans cheered Jackie. The Royals took the lead. Jackie scored the last, winning run.

Jackie was the first Royal to win the league batting crown. His season batting average was .349. He'd scored 113 runs and stolen 40 bases.

Jackie had survived his first Royals season as a hero, but

he had other things on his mind. He and Rachel were about to become parents. Jack Jr. was born in California in November 1946. Jackie spent the holiday with his new family.

He still had a Royals contract. He planned to play basketball during the off-season and then report to spring training in March. Still, he and everyone else in baseball were wondering if and when Branch Rickey would take his experiment to the big leagues.

◄ SIGN MINE!
Jackie signs autographs for Montreal Royals fans, while a batboy patiently waits.

Welcome
to the Big Leagues

he Royals came to Brooklyn to play exhibition games before the start of the 1947 season. Everyone was talking about Jackie Robinson. Jackie knew just when to bunt and when to slam the ball into the outfield. He seemed to have fun as he sneaked

DODGERS
CLUB HOUSE

KEEP OUT

past a baseman for a steal. Other players began to admire his skills.

The Big Day

On April 10 Jackie went to Ebbets Field, the home stadium of the Dodgers, as a Royal. Branch Rickey had him report to the Dodgers' dressing room after the game. He had made it! He was the first African American player in the modern major leagues.

The next day Jackie Robinson covered first base. Rachel and Jack Jr. had just flown in from California. His hard work had paid off. He had broken the color barrier. Jackie was in the big leagues.

Jackie's early days as a Dodger were not easy. A few of the Dodgers had come from the South and kept their southern ideas about race. They didn't want to play with Jackie. They asked Branch Rickey to get rid of him. Of course, Rickey refused.

◀ MOVING ON UP
Robinson, still in his Royals uniform, enters the Dodgers' locker room. He came out of the changing room as a Dodger.

Jackie Remembers

This is how Jackie remembered those first few games:

"At first I was very nervous. But gradually I began to relax and play my game. Sadly, Mr. Rickey's predictions all came true. I was called names by fans and other players—and even by some of my teammates.

"There were insults. There were balls pitched at my head. There were players who deliberately cut me with their spikes. There were death threats. At times, I felt deeply sorry for myself. At times I wondered if being the first Negro in the majors was worth it.

"And at times I wanted to fight back. But I had promised Mr. Rickey that I wouldn't."

The New York fans welcomed Jackie and his exciting way of playing. He kept the pitchers on their toes. And the way he stole bases drove the crowd wild! When the Dodgers went on the road, Jackie was cheered by most black fans and booed by most white fans. Hate letters came in the mail to the Robinsons' home. Jackie had to remind himself again and again to keep his cool.

In Philadelphia the manager of the Phillies led his team in nasty name-calling when Jackie came on the field. The Phillies acted so badly that fans of all races wrote to the Commissioner of Baseball to complain. It was in Philadelphia that the Dodgers began to stand as a team behind Jackie. They respected him for doing his job even when things around him were hard.

Henry "Hank" Aaron, a famed African American

MYSTERY PERSON

☞ **Clue 1:** He played for the Pittsburgh Pirates from 1955–1972.

☞ **Clue 2:** Born in Puerto Rico, he was the first Hispanic ballplayer to be elected to baseball's Hall of Fame.

☞ **Clue 3:** He believed in helping people and once said, "Anytime you have an opportunity to make things better and you don't, you are wasting your time on this Earth."

Can you name this man?

Answer: Roberto Clemente

BASEBALL

Fast Facts

Baseball began in the early 1800s. It came from a game played in England, called rounders. The first game of baseball may have taken place in Hoboken, New Jersey, in 1846. It had four innings instead of nine.

Here are some early rules of baseball. How has the game changed over the years?

Pitches are to be thrown underhanded.

A ball caught on the first bounce is an out.

Players may throw the ball at a runner to put him out.

baseball player who started playing in 1954, wrote about Jackie's early days on the field: "To this day, I don't know how he withstood the things he did without lashing back. I've been through a lot in my time, and I consider myself to be a patient man, but I know I couldn't have done what Jackie did. I don't think anybody else could have done it. Somehow, though, Jackie had the strength to suppress his instincts, to

▼ **NO, YOU DRIVE!**
Jackie and Rachel get the keys to a new car. The car was given to Jackie by Dodgers fans as they honored him with a Jackie Robinson Day in 1947.

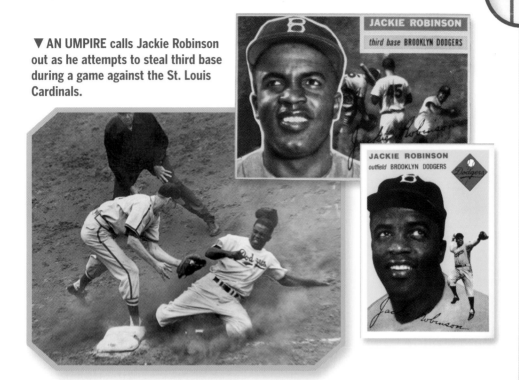

▼ AN UMPIRE calls Jackie Robinson out as he attempts to steal third base during a game against the St. Louis Cardinals.

JACKIE ROBINSON
third base BROOKLYN DODGERS

JACKIE ROBINSON
outfield BROOKLYN DODGERS

sacrifice his pride for his people's. It was an incredible act of selflessness that brought the races closer together than ever before and shaped the dreams of an entire generation."

The 1947 Dodgers became League Champions. Jackie won the Rookie of the Year Award. The Brooklyn fans were so proud that they held a Jackie Robinson Day. Jackie's and Rachel's mothers came to help celebrate. Jackie received many special gifts, including a fancy gold watch and a brand-new Cadillac, one of the finest cars of the time.

It was a wonderful party. The Brooklyn Dodgers had truly taken Jackie Robinson as one of their own.

Opening
Doors for Others

After Jackie, more and more black players joined the major-league baseball teams. Larry Doby was the first in the American League, not long after Jackie.

He played for the Cleveland Indians. Roy Campanella and Don Newcombe joined Jackie with the Dodgers. Jackie Robinson had opened the door, and it stayed open.

In the 1950s doors were opening all over America. Jackie Robinson had given many African Americans the courage to fight for equal rights. He had stopped accepting unfairness in silence. Jackie began to speak out more and more. He wrote a book

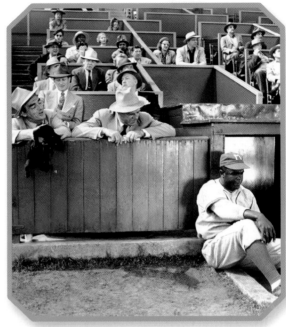

▲ MOVIE STAR
Robinson played himself in the 1950 movie *The Jackie Robinson Story*. In this scene Jackie is being made fun of by fans.

about his life, *The Jackie Robinson Story*. A movie was made from it in 1950. Jackie played himself!

Jackie's major-league career lasted almost ten years, all of them with the Dodgers. The team won six league pennants and a World Series title. The 1956 season

◄ IN 1952 several Negro League players had joined National League teams. These players got together before a spring training game between the Brooklyn Dodgers and Boston Braves. From left are Jackie Robinson, George Crowe, Joe Black, Sam Jethroe, Roy Campanella, and Bill Bruton.

SPORTS FIRSTS

Jackie Robinson once said: "My breakthrough ... paved the way for many fine athletes to come after me." Here are some African American sports firsts.

Basketball: Earl Lloyd of the Washington Capitals was the first African American to play in an NBA game on October 31, 1950.

Tennis: Althea Gibson was the first African American to play in the US Open and the first African American winner in 1957.

Ice Hockey: Willie O'Ree was the first African American to play professional ice hockey. He joined the Boston Bruins in 1958.

Gymnastics: Dominique Dawes was the first African American to win an individual medal (bronze) in gymnastics in the Olympic Games in 1996.

was his last. The Dodgers were moving to California. Jackie found out they were planning to trade him to the New York Giants. But he was already thinking of leaving baseball.

He wasn't as fast as he used to be. He wasn't playing as well as he wished. And by then he and Rachel were the

▼ **TAKING A REST**
Robinson ends his ten-year career with a wave good-bye.

▲ GETTING ALONG
In the 1950s ads such as this one helped promote better relations between people of different colors and religions.

parents of Jack Jr., Sharon, and David. He wanted time with his family.

Jackie announced that he would retire. He was ready to live a life outside baseball.

New Careers

And that's what Jackie Robinson did. He worked in business as a vice president at Chock Full o' Nuts, a coffee company. He wrote a newspaper column. He helped start a bank. Jackie met U.S. presidents and movie stars. He traveled and went deep-sea fishing with his family.

In 1962 he was elected to the Baseball Hall of Fame. The ceremony was held in Cooperstown, New

▲ BACK TO SCHOOL
In 1957 Jackie Robinson (left) and Martin Luther King Jr. received honorary degrees from Howard University.

York. It was one of the proudest days of his life. Two important people from his early years were there to celebrate: his mother, Mallie, and Branch Rickey.

Jackie's concern for opening doors kept him busy. His whole family took part in the 1963 March on Washington for equal rights for African Americans. The Robinsons stood with tens of thousands of Americans of all races to hear Dr. Martin Luther King Jr.'s famous "I Have A Dream" speech.

Jackie believed in Dr. King's words about different races working and living together. That's what his baseball career had been all about. He worked to bring more black managers and coaches to baseball. And he and Rachel raised money to make Dr. King's dreams happen. To do this, they started having "Afternoons of Jazz" concerts each summer in their big backyard in Stamford, Connecticut.

As the children grew up, they helped to plan some of the concerts. Jack Jr. was on his way to his parents' home when he was killed in a car accident in June 1971. Jackie and Rachel somehow pulled together to handle this terrible tragedy.

The family went on. Jackie started a company to build homes for people who didn't have much money.

▼ **HAPPY BIRTHDAY**
Robinson celebrates his thirty-fifth birthday with Rachel and their children. Sharon is on the left, son David is on Dad's knee, and Jackie Jr. is on the right.

Then, in 1972, Jackie died suddenly from a heart attack. Tens of thousands of people lined the streets of New York City to watch his funeral and to say good-bye. Jackie's wide, shining smile would be missed. His pride in being African American would always be admired. His courage and strength—on and off the baseball field—would never be forgotten.

In 1997, fifty years after Jackie Robinson walked out onto Ebbets Field, baseball honored him. The President of the United States, Bill Clinton, came to New York to the Mets' Shea Stadium. The Commissioner of Baseball, Bud Selig, was there. Rachel and Sharon were there, too.

▲ NUMBER 42
Robinson has a place in baseball—and American—history.

applauds Rachel Robinson during ceremonies at Shea Stadium on April 15, 1997. They were celebrating the fiftieth anniversary of Jackie Robinson's breaking major-league baseball's color barrier.

They came together to show that what Jackie did was about more than baseball. It was about making a better world. Jackie's uniform number, 42, was retired forever. Bud Selig said that number 42 belonged to Jackie Robinson "for the ages."

In 2003 the United States Congress voted to give Jackie the Congressional Gold Medal. It's the nation's highest honor.

Many people may still face "closed doors." But Jackie Robinson endured much and fought hard to open them. He was strong inside and out. That's why he will always be a special man—"for the ages."

▲THIS STAMP HONORS Jackie Robinson. He was the first baseball player ever to be honored with his own stamp.

Talking

About Jackie

TIME For Kids editor Jeremy Caplan spoke with Sharon Robinson about her father, Jackie. Here's what she had to say.

▲ Sharon Robinson

Q: *What role did the Negro Leagues play in setting the stage for Jackie Robinson's career?*

A: The Negro Leagues proved that blacks could not only play great professional baseball but could also attract fans. The Negro Leagues gave black players the chance to improve their skills, play at a high level, and be paid for it.

◀ **PLAY BALL!**
Who knows? One day, women may join men on professional baseball teams.

Q: *What were Jackie Robinson's greatest strengths as a person?*
A: He was an incredible husband and a loving father, a concerned citizen and businessman, and a person who fought injustice.

Q: *How did he inspire you?*
A: He taught me to care about others and to believe that social change is possible. He taught me not to be afraid to speak out and stand up for my beliefs. He encouraged me in playing sports. I was an athlete also, and he was supportive of me swimming, skating, skiing, and playing basketball.

Q: *What will he be remembered for?*
A: He will be remembered for his character and his performance as a baseball player.

Jackie Robinson's
Key Dates

1919 Born on January 31, in Cairo, Georgia

1939 Enrolls at UCLA; stars in football and track

1942 Enlists in the United States Army

1945 Signs with Kansas City Monarchs of Negro League; later signs with Brooklyn Dodgers farm team in Montreal

1947 Begins playing for the Dodgers

1949 Wins National League's Most Valuable Player award

1956 Plays final season

1962 Voted into Hall of Fame

1972 Dies on October 24, in Stamford, Connecticut

1927 Philo Taylor Farnsworth invents the television.

1954 The U.S. Supreme Court declares that racial segregation of schools is unconstitutional.

1968 Martin Luther King Jr. is assassinated.